CVR

JAN - - 2009

21st
Century
Skills Library

COOL CAREERS

WILDLIFE
PHOTOGRAPHER

Barbara A. Somervill

Cherry Lake Publishing
Ann Arbor, Michigan

CHERRY
LAKE
Publishing

Published in the United States of America by Cherry Lake Publishing
Ann Arbor, Michigan
www.cherrylakepublishing.com

Content Adviser: Arthur Morris, Wildlife Photographer, Birds As Art

Library of Congress Cataloging-in-Publication Data
Somervill, Barbara A.
Wildlife photographer / by Barbara A. Somervill.
    p. cm.—(Cool careers)
Includes index.
ISBN-13: 978-1-60279-300-2
ISBN-10: 1-60279-300-X
1. Wildlife photography—Vocational guidance—Juvenile literature.
2. Wildlife photographers—Vocational guidance—Juvenile literature. I. Title.
TR729.W54S68 2009
778.9'32023—dc22   2008013722

*Cherry Lake Publishing would like to acknowledge the work of
The Partnership for 21st Century Skills.
Please visit www.21stcenturyskills.org for more information.*

her cubs to be threatened by outsiders. The photographer must be very careful.

After finding the lioness and her cubs, the photographer decides that the best way to get the picture is from behind a nearby tree. She has her equipment ready in a backpack. As quietly as possible, she positions herself behind the tree. She gets her camera ready as the lioness and her cubs come into view. The lioness flops down on her side. Her cubs tumble over her and begin to drink her milk. The photographer aims the camera. She adjusts the light and **focus**. Click! The photographer gets one perfect shot—a lioness tenderly licking her cubs.

Wildlife photography is about more than just fancy cameras and equipment. It is about developing a good photographic eye. Many people over the years have come up with innovative techniques and equipment for taking wildlife pictures.

The first wildlife photographers did not have the equipment to take good action shots of animals.

In 1839, England's Sir John Frederick Herschel first used the word *photography*. The word comes from the Greek words for "light" (*fotizo*) and "writing" (*grafi*). When photography became popular, photographers wanted to take pictures of wild animals in their natural environments. This was not an easy process. Cameras in the mid-1800s required that subjects sit perfectly still. This was difficult, especially for unpredictable wild animals. Early cameras had limited **lenses**, so photographers had to be close to their subject. Lighting was not easy to control. These conditions made early attempts at wildlife photography very hard.

In 1887, brothers Cherry and Richard Kearton of Great Britain headed into the wild. They were armed with a cheap secondhand camera. They wanted to photograph wildlife for a new book. Over the years, Richard wrote the text and Cherry took the photographs for many nature books.

Life & Career Skills

In the United States, one of the earliest nature photographers was William Henry Jackson (1843–1942). When he first became a photographer, Jackson took **portraits** in a small studio in Omaha, Nebraska. This was a short-lived career. He found he preferred to take photos of nature, and he worked hard to develop his skills.

In 1870, Jackson headed into the wilderness of Wyoming. He took photographs of the Green River and Yellowstone Lake. His self-direction and persistence helped him become a great photographer. His photographs helped convince Congress to declare Yellowstone the first national park in March 1872.

Early cameras were not as easy to carry around as today's models.

Their first work was titled *British Birds, Nests, and Egg Collecting.*

Cherry Kearton became the first "big game" photographer. He produced flash photography of a lion and a rhino. Over the years, he traveled to India, Borneo, Canada, and Africa. On his trips, he took pictures of wildlife in still photographs and early films. His best-selling book, *The Island of Penguins,* showed photos of African penguins and ordinary people.

In those early days, all photos were black and white. Cameras were bulky boxes with a single lens. Film was a flat piece of prepared glass, called a plate. Photography was heavy, clumsy, and stiff. But all of that would change. People began experimenting with ways to make clearer, better photographs.

In 1859, the first **panoramic** camera came into use. This invention allowed photographers to produce wide images. These were helpful when taking pictures of places such as the Grand Canyon. During the 1880s, George Eastman worked on many inventions. In 1884, he invented flexible, paper-based film. Four years later, Eastman developed a camera that used roll film—not too different from film that can be used in cameras today. Color film, an invention of Eastman's Kodak Company, did not appear until 1935.

Improvements in cameras, lenses, and film came quickly. A camera that could produce "instant" pictures—the Polaroid camera—appeared in 1948. Six years later, Kodak introduced high-speed film.

Today, digital cameras have made quality photography instantaneous. The first digital camera was introduced by Canon in 1979. Improvements to digital cameras have made them cheaper, better, and easier to use. Digital cameras require no film. They have built-in computers that record pictures in **pixels**. Digital pictures can be downloaded to a computer. The photograph's lighting or **contrast** can be improved by using a software program to "fix" errors.

Improved equipment has allowed wildlife photographers to take shots of cheetahs on the run, dolphins spinning in air, and hummingbirds hovering near flowers. A wildlife photographer uses these tools to take and develop amazing wildlife pictures.

CHAPTER TWO

WORKING ON THE WILD SIDE

A day in the life of a wildlife photographer often includes carrying equipment from one location to the next.

The day begins very early for a wildlife photographer. The photographer gets up an hour or two before sunrise, when wild animals are most active. He makes sure all the equipment is in working order. He finds a site to take pictures.

The photographer then sets up his equipment before the animals are moving around.

It can be very hot and uncomfortable inside a blind.

Taking a shot may require building a blind. This is a place to hide so that the animals do not notice you. This is especially helpful when photographing birds. One clever photographer made a floating blind covered with reeds and tree bark so he could take photos of ducks and geese on ponds.

Wildlife photography begins with the subject and its environment. An eagle in a cage is not a good photo subject. An eagle in the wild catching a fish in its talons makes for a better subject. Wildlife photographers must know everything there is to know about their subjects—where to find them and how they live. They must go where the animals live. They think about the shape and size of the animal. A long animal—a cheetah—requires a landscape, or **horizontal**, shot. A tall animal—a giraffe—needs a portrait, or **vertical**, shot.

Wild animals naturally prefer places that are not convenient for humans. Wildlife photographers must deal with the inconvenience of traveling. This requires a lot of patience. Finding an animal requires patience. Getting the right shot requires patience. Patience is a very important characteristic for photographers.

Wildlife photographers sometimes use helicopters for transportation.
They can also be used to take photos of animals from above.

Photographers also understand light. Taking images at dawn or sunset might provide stunning colors in the sky. The subject might appear in silhouette—a black outline against a vivid background. Photographers also use filters to help control light.

Most professional wildlife photographers specialize in animal species that interest them. Some photograph

African animals, while others photograph only insects. Some may prefer birds, sea creatures, or snakes. Being an expert on penguins, for example, might get a photographer an assignment to the Galapagos Islands or even Antarctica. Photographers' interests may determine where they work.

Finally, wildlife photographers must always consider the animal. They should always put the welfare of the animal first. Most photographers would never do anything that would threaten the safety of the animal or its young just to take a picture.

21st Century Content

British nature photographer Nigel Dennis was asked which photo he was most honored to have published. This was his choice:

"A while back, I got a whole bundle of tear sheets from my [English] agent. Among them was a poster that was given away in a Polish children's magazine. The picture was a Verreaux's Sifaka (lemur). For sure, all over Poland, kids had my picture of a lemur on their bedroom walls—but the chances are they may never get to see a real lemur in Madagascar. I thought this was great and it really meant a lot to me."

The pictures that photographers take are shared all over the world today. Magazines such as *National Geographic* give photographers a global audience. The Internet makes it easy for photographers to share their work with anyone who has access to a computer.

Photographers are willing to get into uncomfortable positions to get interesting shots.

Today, the wildlife photographer has trekked through the rain forests of Papua New Guinea. His assignment is to take images of birds of paradise doing their mating dances. He drove the first 60 miles (100 kilometers) and hiked the next 15 miles (24 km). He set up base camp six days ago. He built a blind on the second day. For the past four days, he has been cooped up in the blind. Unfortunately, the subject of the pictures he was waiting to take did not show up.

Wild animals do not pose for pictures. They do not always appear where they are expected. Even if the photographer finds the perfect spot to wait, the animals may not cooperate. Some photographers spend days, weeks, or even months trying to get the perfect shot.

The sun rises, and the day grows hotter. Boredom sets in. It would be nice to stretch and walk around. Hunger begins to set in. Unfortunately, lunch today will be an apple, a granola bar, and a bottle of water. The photographer does not want to leave the blind. Who knows when the opportunity for the perfect shot will come along?

The sun has nearly set. The photographer is tired and just about to stop working for the day. Suddenly, a bird of

Photographing animals, such as this bird of paradise, can require a lot of patience.

paradise lands in the clearing. The bird begins dancing to attract a mate. The photographer takes a few photos. Then a noise startles the bird and it flies away. The photographer has waited nearly four full days and was only able to take photos for less than one minute!

After an hour's hike back to camp, the photographer connects the camera to his laptop computer. He downloads the shots and smiles. On the screen is the perfect shot—a male bird of paradise in full display. The photo is sharp and clear and will earn a large fee.

After putting in a 16-hour workday, it is time for bed. For wildlife photographers, the days are long. Tomorrow, the photographer will hike out of the jungle, load up his Land Rover, and head home to prepare for the next assignment. What is the next project? It is taking photos of polar bears in the Hudson Bay region of Canada. For wildlife photographers, the adventure never ends!

CHAPTER THREE

TRAINING AND EQUIPMENT

Professional photographers must stay informed about the latest technologies. These students are learning about digital photography.

Wildlife photographers should have a combination of skills and talent. They should also be loving and respectful of animals in their natural habitats. Today's photographer must understand the art of photography. Photographers who use digital cameras must learn how to use photo-editing software. They must also know how to run a business.

Photography schools, art schools, colleges, and technical schools offer photography classes and workshops. These classes teach people how to use cameras and lenses. They also teach photo **composition** and film developing. Photography classes usually begin with using black-and-white film and learning the basics.

Most photographers have regular jobs in studios. Wildlife photographers must go into the wild to photograph their subjects. Most of these photographers do not have regular jobs working for one

One good way to learn how to take photos is at a wildlife photography workshop. These workshops are held worldwide. Most workshops teach people how to photograph specific types of animals. Many professional nature photographers teach others their skills in these workshops. If you are interested in nature photography, a workshop can give you a taste of what a career in wildlife photography might be like. What kinds of animals are you interested in photographing? What do you think you can do now to prepare for a career as a wildlife photographer?

Some lenses allow photographers to get excellent images from a distance.

company. They sell their work to magazines and other clients on a **freelance** basis.

There are two ways for a freelance photographer to sell photographs. The first way is to get an assignment in advance. This does not happen very often. More commonly, photographers sell their images through companies that sell the work of many different photographers. Most professionals use both methods to earn money. Freelance work is not easy. Freelancers are always working hard to sell their images. The hours are long, and a freelancer has to earn enough money to live on.

Wildlife photographers need plenty of equipment. Equipment is not cheap. One good-quality camera body might cost more than $5,000! Lenses can cost more. Digital cameras require computers and software. For traveling, everything must be protected in padded cases, and the cases themselves are costly.

The minimum amount of equipment needed is a camera body, a variety of lenses, a tripod, and filters. If you're not using a digital camera, you will need film, too. Lenses magnify the view. They let the photographer take a close-up picture from a distance. A tripod is a three-legged stand for keeping the camera and lens still. Without one, the picture's focus will not be as sharp.

A photographer places the gear on the tripod, focuses, and takes the photograph.

But expensive equipment is not enough to guarantee a perfect shot every time. A photographer's artistic eye, training, and experience are even more important. A photographer who doesn't have those things won't be able to take brilliant pictures that dazzle the eye.

CHAPTER FOUR

A FUTURE IN PHOTOGRAPHY

Traveling to faraway places can be exciting. But it also means spending time away from family and friends.

Wildlife photography is not a career for people who enjoy living in comfort. While a photographer's home may be comfortable, the work environment is rugged and demanding. Sometimes it is even dangerous.

One way to break into this field is by taking workshops with professionals. Another way is to get to

Learning & Innovation Skills

Wildlife photographers never stop learning. They can use what they learn about one animal for later projects. For example, a photographer studying and photographing elephant seals will discover that these animals come onto beaches to mate. If the photographer gets an assignment about walruses, some of the knowledge learned about elephant seals comes in handy. Walruses also mate on land—and they gather in herds, much like elephant seals. Wildlife photographers apply what they learn to new situations.

know people in the field. Many wildlife photographers need assistants and will train someone who is truly interested in photography.

One problem that wildlife photographers face is getting access to take photos of endangered or threatened animals. Often, photographers will be working outside their home nation. They must contact government authorities and get permission to take photographs in their countries. Other places are difficult to access because of weather. For example, photo assignments in polar regions are not easy to arrange. Travel and weather conditions create problems. A photographer must learn how to exist

*Photographers who work underwater must learn
how to safely use diving equipment.*

in such a place. Access is limited because the environment
is dangerous.

Taking images of underwater animals can be very
expensive. Photographers need a boat, diving gear, and
underwater photography equipment. Boating and diving
require a crew for safety and support.

In today's digital world, a photographer must keep
up with the latest trends in equipment. Advances in

camera bodies and lenses occur all the time. Digital equipment improves, and software changes regularly. A professional needs to keep up with all the trends, yet buy new equipment wisely. Photographers must learn how to properly use this new equipment, and feel comfortable with it, so that the quality of work stays the same.

Wildlife photographers deal with arctic cold, scorching desert heat, torrential rains, floods, and some very uncomfortable places. They work on the ice and sand, on top of sharp rocks, in trees, from hot air balloons, and underwater. They face charging bears, hissing snakes, curious apes, and biting insects. And yet, most wildlife photographers wouldn't have it any other way. They love being part of nature and bringing nature into people's lives. The thing that matters most is getting that one perfect shot . . . click!

SOME FAMOUS WILDLIFE PHOTOGRAPHERS

Heather Angel (1941–) has been a leader in the field of wildlife photography for more than 25 years. She has provided photography for nearly 50 books, including *Giant Pandas, How to Succeed in Wildlife Photography,* and *Animal Photography.*

Nigel Dennis (1953–) moved to Africa in 1985, hoping to make wildlife photography a full-time job. At first, he worked as a salesman and used his free time doing wildlife photography. Finally, in 1991, he went full time as a photographer.

Frans Lanting (1951–) is currently a photographer-in-residence for *National Geographic* magazine. Lanting's books include *Jungles, Penguin, Living Planet, Eye to Eye, Okavango: Africa's Last Eden,* and *Forgotten Edens.* Lanting has won many awards, including BBC Wildlife Photograph of the Year and the Sierra Club's Ansel Adams Award.

Tom Mangelsen (1946–) published his first book in 1989, called *Images of Nature: The Photographs of Thomas D. Mangelsen.* In 1994, he was named Wildlife Photographer of the Year. In 2000, American Photo Magazine named him one of the 100 Most Important People in Photography.

Flip Nicklin (1948–) is often called the best whale photographer in the world. He is an underwater photographer who has made more than 5,500 dives. He can free dive (with no scuba gear) to 90 feet (27 meters) deep.

Andy Rouse (1965–) specializes in animal species that are particularly dangerous or hard to find. He has shot tigers in India, grizzly bears in Alaska, and baby harp seals in the Arctic. He has published a book on techniques of photographing mammals in the wild.

Glossary

composition (kom-puh-ZISH-uhn) the arrangement of the elements in an image

contrast (KAHN-trast) the difference between light and dark in a photo or picture

focus (FOH-kuhss) the sharpness of a picture, or the act of adjusting a camera to get a sharp picture

freelance (FREE-lanss) done by a person who hires out services on a job-to-job basis

horizontal (hor-uh-ZON-tuhl) aligned along the horizon, or side to side

lenses (LENZ-iz) pieces of equipment that draw light into the camera and focus the light for the shot

panoramic (pan-uh-RAM-ik) a wide view, such as a landscape

pixels (PIKS-uhlz) minute areas of light on a computer display screen that make up a picture

portraits (POR-trayts) pictures of a person or animal

vertical (VUR-tuh-kuhl) oriented up and down, such as a tree or a skyscraper

For More Information

Books

Gaines, Thom. *Digital Photo Madness: 50 Weird & Wacky Things to Do with Your Camera*. New York: Lark Books, 2006.

Thomas, William David. *Wildlife Photographer*. Pleasantville, NY: Gareth Stevens Publishing, 2008.

Web Sites

BetterPhoto.com—Tricks for Pet Photography
www.betterphoto.com/article.asp?id=76
Find hints for taking better photos of your pets

Nature Photographers Online Magazine
www.naturephotographers.net/
Read the magazine that nature photographers read

Serengeti Photo Safari
www.pbs.org/wnet/nature/serengeti/multimedia/serengeti-game.html
Play an online photo safari game

INDEX

ABOUT THE AUTHOR

Barbara A. Somervill writes children's nonfiction books on a variety of topics. As a writer, she has had many different cool careers—teacher, news reporter, author, scriptwriter, and restaurant critic. She believes that researching new and different topics makes writing every book an adventure. When she is not writing, Ms. Somervill plays duplicate bridge, reads avidly, and travels.